THE ENGLISH IN AMERICA

The IN AMERICA *Series*

Lerner Publications Company
241 First Avenue North, Minneapolis, Minnesota 55401

The IN AMERICA *Series*

THE **ENGLISH** IN AMERICA

EDWIN H. CATES

Published by

Lerner Publications Company

Minneapolis, Minnesota

ACKNOWLEDGMENTS

The illustrations are reproduced through the courtesy of: pp. 6, 17 (top and bottom), 18 (top left and right), 21, 27, 32 (left), 33 (left), 48 (top, center, bottom), 51 (left), 52 (top, center, bottom), 53 (top and bottom), 62 (top left), 64, 65 (top left and right), Library of Congress; pp. 8, 15, 19 (left), 22, 24, 29, 32 (right), 35, 50, 51 (right and bottom), Independent Picture Service; pp. 12, 14, 16 (bottom), 61, The Smithsonian Institution; p. 16 (top), United States Department of Interior; p. 18 (bottom), Enoch Pratt Free Library, Baltimore; pp. 19 (right), 20, 65 (bottom), 67, Post Office Department, Division of Philately; p. 28, New England Mutual Life Insurance Company; p. 30, British Museum; pp. 31 (left and right), 59, The Pennsylvania Academy of the Fine Arts; pp. 33 (right), 47 (left), Independence National Historical Park Collection; p. 40, United States Immigration and Naturalization Service; p. 44, The Virginia Museum of Fine Arts; p. 46, National Gallery of Art; p. 47 (right), Amherst College; p. 54 (top), Harry S. Truman Library; p. 54 (center), Minnesota Democrat-Farmer-Labor Party; p. 54 (bottom), The White House; p. 56 (top), United States Navy; p. 56 (bottom left), Houghton Library, Harvard University; p. 56 (bottom right), Nancy Crampton for Farrar, Straus, and Giroux, Inc.; p. 58 (left), The Metropolitan Museum of Art; p. 58 (right), Brown University Library; p. 62 (top right), Singer Sewing Machine Company; pp. 62 (bottom left and right), 63 (top left and right), North Carolina Travel Information Division; p. 63 (bottom), Edison Electric Institute; p. 66, Wide World Photos; p. 68 (left), American Red Cross; p. 68 (right), Wallace Kirkland; p. 69 (top left), Station KSTP, Minneapolis; p. 69 (top center), Collectors Book Store, Hollywood; p. 69 (top right), TV Times; p. 69 (bottom), Arnold Newman for Alfred A. Knopf.

The Library of Congress cataloged the
original printing of this title as follows:

Cates, Edwin H.
   The English in America [by] Edwin H. Cates. Minneapolis,
Lerner Publications Co. [1966]

   70 p. illus., ports. 24 cm. (The In America series)

   Contents: The background of English colonization in America.—The English colonial period in American history.—English immigration to the United States.—Contributions of English-Americans.

   1. British in the U. S.—Juvenile literature. I. Title.

E184.B7C3   301.45342073   66-5730
ISBN 0-8225-0205-4 [Library]   MARC
ISBN 0-8225-1007-3 [Paper]

1986 Revised Edition

International Standard Book Number: 0-8225-0205-4 Library Edition
International Standard Book Number: 0-8225-1007-3 Paper Edition

Library of Congress Catalog Card Number: AC 66-10145

8   9   10   94   93   92   91   90   89   88   87   86

...CONTENTS...

The Cabots reach the coast of North America. In 1497 and 1498, an Italian captain, John Cabot, and his son, Sebastian, explored the coast of North America from Newfoundland to South Carolina. They were in the service of Henry VII, King of England. Although England made no further attempts at exploration or settlement until 1578, her claim to North American territory rested on the voyage of the Cabots.

PART I.

The Background of English Colonization in America

1. *England Lags in Colonization*

Shortly after Columbus discovered America in 1492, Spain began to establish a colonial empire in the New World. By 1580, this included the West Indies, South America, Central America, and the southern portion of North America. Between 1534 and 1600, France established a large colony in eastern and central North America. This consisted of the St. Lawrence Valley, the region around Lake Superior, and the northern part of the Ohio Valley. In contrast with these achievements, England lagged behind Spain and France for many years in colonization in America. Not until the year 1607, 115 years after Columbus' first voyage, did a permanent English colony appear in the New World.

England's delay in colonization was due to four unfavorable conditions. First, her territory, population, and wealth were all smaller than those of France and Spain. Second, for many years England's naval strength was weaker than that of Spain and France. Third, no English ruler prior to 1558 was interested in overseas colonization. Fourth, for most of the 16th century England's attention was occupied with internal problems.

Not until near the end of Queen Elizabeth's reign, 1558-1603, did England possess the means, or tools, for successful colonization in America. These were a strong navy, enough money for foreign investment, and thousands of individuals willing to settle overseas. The English Navy grew rapidly under Queen Elizabeth. It was so strong in 1588 that it completely destroyed a large

Queen Elizabeth ruled England from 1558 to 1603. It was during her reign that the Spanish Armada was defeated and a new interest in exploration and settlement in the New World was aroused. Elizabeth granted Humphrey Gilbert and Walter Raleigh charters to found colonies in America, but both men were unsuccessful.

Spanish fleet, called the Spanish Armada, which tried to attack England. This victory made England the leading naval power of the world. A profitable trade was soon opened with northern Europe, and a rich merchant class appeared in England. In spite of this prosperity, however, thousands of Englishmen lived in poverty because of changing practices in land ownership. These people soon began to demand overseas colonies where they could begin life anew.

2. *The Search for Profits and New Land*

About the year 1600, wealthy English merchants began to seek new places to invest their money. It was common knowledge that Spain and France had made large profits from their American possessions. Thus, English colonies in the New World appealed to English merchants as a sound commercial venture.

In 1606, this plan took shape when a group of traders, who lived in London, organized a trading society to establish a colony in America. Money for this project was raised by selling shares of stock to anyone who wished to buy. The merchant class and any of the well-to-do who bought this stock expected to earn a large return on their investment. A colony was planned which would produce a variety of goods and articles that could be sold at a handsome profit throughout western Europe as well as in England. The colonists who were to settle in America would be poor men. The company would transport them to the New World and give each settler one share of stock for his time and labor. During the summer of 1606, King James I granted the London Company, as it was called, a charter to found a colony along the Atlantic coast of North America. In December 1606, the London Company sent out a group of 120 prospective colonists.

3. *Hard Times in England*

While foreign trade made many English merchants wealthy in the closing years of Elizabeth's reign, most of the poorer class experienced hard times and unemployment. Hard times were caused by a sharp rise in the cost of living. Between 1540 and 1600, an immense quantity of gold and silver reached Europe from the Spanish colonies in America. Part of this new wealth reached England through payments in foreign trade. This caused a sudden rise in prices throughout England. The laboring class did not earn enough to meet this increase in prices, and a great deal of hardship and suffering occurred.

At this same time, extensive unemployment was spreading throughout England. During the last 10 years of Elizabeth's reign, England found a very profitable market for raw wool in Flanders, or present-day Belgium, which lay just across the English Channel. To take advantage of this opportunity, many English landowners began to raise large herds of sheep. Previously, England's agricultural land had been tilled by thousands of small tenant farmers. These farmers were now pushed off the land and their place was taken by a few shepherds tending large flocks. There were no other jobs in which to employ these idle farmers. Many became thieves or beggars. Severe laws were passed against idleness and non-payment of debts. Prisons soon became overcrowded, and many leaders in public life demanded that foreign colonies be established for this excess population.

4. *Political and Religious Conflict*

As a ruler, Queen Elizabeth was very popular and beloved by her subjects. She ruled with immense personal power, but she was always careful to consult Parliament on all major problems.

In 1603, Queen Elizabeth died. She was followed on the English throne by King James I. He was arrogant, proud, and desired complete power. Early in his reign, James I announced that he would be answerable only to God for his conduct as king. This claim was new in English history, and it was deeply resented by the English people who had come to consider Parliament as a basic part of the English government.

Long before the reign of James I, Parliament had gained the right to levy taxes, and to limit the royal income to an annual grant of money. During the first year that James was king, he quarreled bitterly with Parliament over the amount he received. In anger, James I refused to call Parliament into session for a number of years. This compelled the king to levy illegal taxes of his own. These consisted of forced loans, or "donations," which were placed especially on the wealthy members of Parliament. These highhanded acts and claims of James I aroused widespread discontent throughout England.

In addition to political disputes, religious quarrels and discontent caused many Englishmen to settle in America. In the year 1534, the English king, Henry VIII, had cut all formal religious ties between England and the Church of Rome. A new religious denomination, the Church of England, or the Anglican Church as it was commonly called, was established by an act of Parliament. From then on, all Englishmen were required by law to belong to and support this church.

During the reign of Queen Elizabeth, a group of reformers appeared in England who felt that the Anglican Church did not differ sufficiently from the Church of Rome. This group, called the "Puritans," wished to purify the Church of England of many customs and practices handed down from the Roman Catholic faith. A majority of the Puritans hoped to reform the Anglican

Church. A small radical group existed, however, called the "Separatists," which wanted to establish a new church of its own.

James I proved to be as much a tyrant in religion as he was in politics. He demanded complete loyalty to the Church of England from every Englishman. He disliked the Puritans, and he persecuted them with many harsh penalties. James I especially hated the Separatists, and the cruelest penalties were reserved for them. In 1609, the members of one Separatist congregation fled to Holland to escape royal persecution. In 1620, members of this same group, who had taken the name of "Pilgrims," moved from Holland to America and established a colony in New England.

King James I died in 1625. Both the leaders of Parliament and the Puritans throughout England hoped that the new king, Charles I, would be more lenient. However, they were keenly disappointed. Charles I soon proved to be even more tyrannical than James I. Many Puritans, and supporters of Parliament, now became discouraged. Charles I was very young, and he might reign for many years. A large number of Puritans believed that it would be best to leave England. In 1629, a group of several thousand organized an expedition to New England, and in 1630 they founded a new colony in that part of America.

A coin issued to honor the 350th anniversary of Sir Walter Raleigh's colony on Roanoke Island, North Carolina. Raleigh spent his personal fortune in several unsuccessful attempts to found a colony in America.

PART II.

The English Colonial Period in American History

1. *The Lost Colony*

The first attempt to establish an English colony in the New World ended in failure. This project resulted from the interest of Sir Humphrey Gilbert in the geography of North America. Gilbert was certain that a Northwest Passage to the Orient lay somewhere in a southeast-northwest direction through the North American continent. He believed that an English colony founded on the Atlantic coast would aid in the search for this passage.

In the year 1578, Gilbert secured a charter from Queen Elizabeth which authorized him to found a colony anywhere along the Atlantic coast not occupied by another European power. England's claim to this part of North America was based on an earlier voyage in 1497 by an Italian sailor named John Cabot who had been sent out by King Henry VII. Actually, Sir Humphrey Gilbert did not accomplish a great deal. In the summer of 1578, he led an expedition to the Carolina coast, but this was soon chased back to England by a larger Spanish fleet. One of Gilbert's ships was commanded by a half-brother, Walter Raleigh, who was only 26 years old.

The reverse side of the Roanoke Island commemorative coin shows Virginia Dare, the first white child born in North America.

Five years later, in 1583, Gilbert attempted to found a colony in Newfoundland, well north of Spanish interference. Gilbert's ship was lost at sea, however, and the expedition ended in failure. Young Walter Raleigh became anxious to carry on Gilbert's activities. In 1584 he was given a charter by Queen Elizabeth to establish a colony of his own in America. Raleigh sent out two ships to find a good site for a colony on Chesapeake Bay. The captain of this expedition thought that Roanoke Island on the Carolina coast would be a better location. Several times in 1585 and 1586 groups of colonists landed on Roanoke Island, but each time the colony was abandoned for one reason or another.

Finally, in May 1587, Walter Raleigh, now Sir Walter Raleigh after being knighted by Queen Elizabeth, made a major effort to found a colony in America. He sent out three ships with 150 prospective colonists, 25 of whom were women and children. To equip this expedition, Raleigh spent the last of his personal fortune of some 400,000 pounds, a huge sum in those days. The captain of the expedition disobeyed Raleigh's orders and landed the colonists on Roanoke Island instead of along Chesapeake Bay. Then, with two of the three vessels, he abandoned the colonists and sailed back to England.

By the end of August, supplies were exhausted and the leader of the colony, John White, left for England in the one remaining ship. He reached England a few months before the attack by the Spanish Armada, and he was detained by the authorities. It was not until 1591 that White was able to return to Roanoke Island to find out what happened to the colonists. He discovered that the island was deserted, and the fort in ruins. From then on the Roanoke settlement was referred to as the "Lost Colony." The real fate of the colonists was never known. They may have been killed by hostile natives, but it seems more likely that they found refuge with a friendly tribe of Indians who lived nearby.

2. *The Founding of 13 English Colonies*

Though Gilbert and Raleigh failed to establish a colony in America, they showed the difficulties of colonization. Their efforts also interested others in trying to establish a settlement. Twenty years after the Lost Colony disappeared an English settlement was founded along the Atlantic coast. This began a program of colonization which placed 13 English colonies in America between the years 1607 and 1733.

The first permanent English colony in America was named Virginia. It was founded by settlers sent by the London Company

"The Lost Colony." John White, leader of the Roanoke Island colony, left for England in 1587. When he returned in 1591, he found only the name "Croatoan," an Indian tribe, carved on a tree. The colonists had disappeared. It is believed that the settlers were killed. They may have found refuge with friendly Indians.

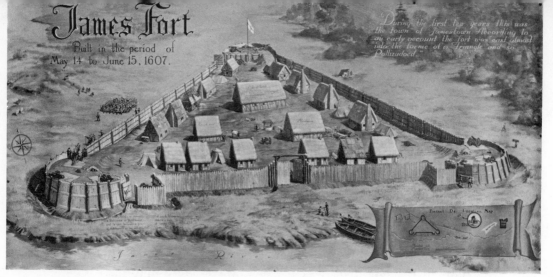

James Fort

Built in the period of
May 14 to June 15, 1607.

During the first ten years this was
the town of Jamestown. According to
an early account the fort was cast almost
into the forme of a Triangle and so
Pallizadoed.

The reconstruction of James Fort, the settlement known as Jamestown. It was started May 14, 1607, by settlers of the London Company.

in December 1606. Early in May 1607, these settlers landed on the northern bank of the James River, in present-day Virginia, 35 miles inland from the sea. Of the 120 prospective colonists who had left England, only 104 survived the voyage. The sole purpose of this colony was to earn a profit for the stockholders of the London Company.

The next English colony established was named Plymouth. It was located on the southeastern coast of New England. This colony was founded for religious rather than commercial purposes. The settlers who founded Plymouth were the Separatists who had fled from England to Holland in 1609. Unhappy over conditions they

The Pilgrim half-dollar, issued in honor of the 300th anniversary of the landing of the Pilgrims at Plymouth. Governor William Bradford (left) was the leader of the Pilgrims. His *History of the Plymouth Plantation* is our main source of information about the lives of these early settlers. The reverse side (right) shows the *Mayflower*, which carried 102 passengers and a crew of 47.

The signing of the Mayflower Compact on November 11, 1620, at Provincetown Bay. Before leaving the ship, Pilgrim leaders signed a compact agreeing to make and obey laws ". . . from time to time, as shall be thought most meet and convenient for the general Good of the Colony."

found in Holland, the Separatists decided to settle in America. On December 21, 1620, about 100 members of this group landed in New England. They named their first village, and their colony, Plymouth. These colonists became known as the Pilgrims.

The third English colony was Massachusetts Bay. The founders of this colony were Puritans who had become discouraged over the prospect of a long tyrannical reign by Charles I. In 1629-1630, plans were made for an expedition, and more than 2,000 Puritans sailed for America. They landed on the eastern coast of New England. Boston soon became the major city and capital of this new Puritan colony.

The Puritans who founded Massachusetts Bay colony wished to enjoy religious liberty, but they had no interest in granting such

Pilgrims going to church. The Pilgrims, members of a Separatist congregation, fled first to Holland and then to America in search of religious freedom.

Roger Williams, a Puritan minister who was banished from Massachusetts Bay Colony, founded Rhode Island. Williams fought for individual liberty in both government and religion.

Thomas Hooker's emigration to Connecticut. Reverend Hooker and his followers left Massachusetts Bay and founded their own colony in the fertile Connecticut Valley.

liberty to others. Anyone who disagreed with Puritan beliefs and practices was persecuted. In 1635, two Puritan clergymen, Reverend Roger Williams and Reverend Thomas Hooker, who expressed liberal opinions, were expelled from the colony. The following year, both of these men helped found new colonies in New England. Reverend Williams established the colony of Rhode Island and Reverend Hooker created the colony of Connecticut. New Hampshire, the northern section of New England, became a colony in 1679 after enough settlers moved into that area.

Meanwhile, in 1634, the colony of Maryland was founded on Chesapeake Bay, several hundred miles south of New England. It

Cecil Calvert, known as Lord Baltimore, founded the colony of Maryland as a haven for English Catholics, but granted religious toleration to all settlers.

18

was established by Cecil Calvert, a nobleman known as Lord Baltimore. Calvert was a member of the Roman Catholic Church. This denomination was then being persecuted in England, and Calvert founded Maryland to serve as a haven for Catholics in the New World.

The Society of Friends, or Quakers, was also persecuted in England at that time. A prominent English Quaker, William Penn, sought to aid the Quakers and established a colony for them in America. The king at that time, Charles II, had earlier borrowed a considerable sum of money from Penn's father, Admiral Penn of the English Navy. After the death of Admiral Penn, William Penn agreed to cancel this debt in return for a charter from Charles II granting Penn the right to found a colony. In 1682, Penn arrived in America and began the task of establishing the colony of Pennsylvania. Within a few years, this became the largest and most prosperous English colony in North America.

Since the 1620's, the Hudson Valley in present-day New York had belonged to Holland. As a Dutch colony, it had been known as New Netherland. The neighboring English colonies were jealous of its rich fur trade. The English also disliked this colony because it divided New England from the other English colonies farther

The Duke of York, brother of King Charles II. The Duke sent an army and fleet to America in 1664. The Dutch settlers quickly surrendered New Netherlands to the English.

The William Penn commemorative stamp, issued in 1932, marked the 250th anniversary of the arrival of the great English reformer in America.

south. In 1664, England's patience gave out, and a fleet was sent to demand the surrender of New Netherland. The Dutch colonists, lacking an army or navy, gave in without firing a shot. Charles II renamed the colony New York after his brother, the Duke of York.

In 1663, a group of eight English nobles were given a charter by Charles II to establish a colony between Virginia and Spanish Florida. The result was a colony called Carolina. Later, in 1711, it was divided into two colonies known as North Carolina and South Carolina.

Shortly after 1650, small groups of Dutch, Swedish, and Swiss colonists settled along the Atlantic coast between New York and Maryland. In the 1680's and 1690's, larger numbers of English settlers moved into this area, and in 1702 the region was organized as the colony of New Jersey.

The last English colony to be founded along the Atlantic coast was Georgia. It was established by James Oglethorpe to serve as a haven for Englishmen who had been imprisoned for non-payment of debts. At that time, it was a common practice to imprison men, often for many years, for failure to pay all debts, however small. In 1733, Oglethorpe led 100 settlers, chiefly ex-debtors, to begin the colonization of Georgia. The city of Savannah was soon founded and became the capital of the new colony. The prison authorities in England refused, however, to cooperate with Oglethorpe after he reached Georgia and very few debtors were sent out to increase the population of the colony.

A three-cent stamp issued in 1933 to honor General Oglethorpe and commemorate the 250th anniversary of the settlement of Georgia.

English sailing ship. The small vessels used in colonial times made the voyages to America long, difficult, and dangerous.

3. *The Difficulties of Colonization*

The English colonists who settled in America during the first century of colonization had to face many harsh and unfavorable conditions. First, the voyage from England itself was long, uncomfortable, and very dangerous. An average crossing lasted about three months. Ships were always overcrowded. Disease frequently caused the death of some passengers. Food and water supplies often became low, or completely exhausted. Storms were especially dangerous because they could easily destroy the small ships of that time.

Those who survived the passage from England soon faced other difficulties. Malaria was a constant source of illness and death to those who settled along the sluggish tidewater rivers and on the coastal marshes of Virginia. In the Carolinas and Georgia, a variety of tropical fevers and diseases plagued the early colonists. In both the Virginia and Plymouth colonies, the first settlers experienced severe famine until they learned how to grow the local crops. Friendly Indian tribes helped to solve this problem. In the New England colonies, the long hard winters took a heavy toll of life. In New England, too, the rocky soil made farming difficult except in the Connecticut Valley and Massachusetts Bay colonies. In all

The English, like other settlers, were continually threatened by Indians. In 1622, 400 settlers in Virginia were killed. In 1644, 300 more died in Indian warfare.

the colonies south of New England, dense forests made clearing the land for agriculture a long and difficult task.

As a rule, the Indians were a constant and dangerous threat to the English colonists. They bitterly resented the westward expansion of white settlement. The whole colonial era was filled with almost continual Indian warfare. In some periods, the danger was worse than in others. For instance, in 1622, the population of Virginia was nearly wiped out by an Indian massacre. In the 1670's, the New England colonies barely survived an attack by an Indian Confederation, and in the 1760's, the whole colonial frontier was driven back about 100 miles, across the Appalachian Mountains, by a great alliance of the Indian tribes of the Ohio Valley.

4. The Numbers of English Immigrants

The first efforts by Englishmen at colonization in America were made on a very small scale. The colony of Virginia, for example, was established by 104 settlers. Plymouth colony was founded by less than 100 Pilgrims. Maryland was planted by Cecil

Calvert and approximately 100 fellow Catholics. Georgia was begun by James Oglethorpe and about 100 English debtors. William Penn and slightly more than 100 Quakers organized the colony of Pennsylvania.

Only two English colonies were established by a larger number of settlers. These were Massachusetts Bay and New York. Massachusetts Bay Colony was founded by 2,000 English Puritans in 1630. New York, which had previously been the Dutch colony of New Netherland, already had a population of 10,000 when it became an English possession in 1664.

The reasons which forced and attracted Englishmen to settle in America in the early 1600's continued during the entire colonial period. This caused a constant rise in the colonial population. Fourteen thousand colonists settled in Virginia between 1607 and 1624. The population of Maryland increased from several hundred in 1634 to 8,000 in 1657; Georgia from a scant 100 in 1733 to 9,000 in 1760; Massachusetts Bay from 2,000 in 1630 to 16,000 in 1643. Both of the Carolina colonies experienced a continual rise in population. In 1717, the population of North Carolina was 9,000. By 1760, this figure had grown to 93,000. In the same period, the population of South Carolina increased from 19,000 to 100,000. Other colonies such as Pennsylvania, New Jersey, and Delaware enjoyed a similar growth of population in this period due to immigration. Pennsylvania and New Jersey received a larger total of non-English immigrants than any of the other colonies.

By 1690, the population of the English colonies in America stood at 220,000. By 1760, this figure had risen to 1,500,000. In 1790, seven years after the colonies obtained independence, the United States had a population of more than 2,750,000 persons. The great majority of this population was English in descent.

English Population in America — 1790		
	Number of People in Each State of English Origin	Percent of Total Population
Maryland	175,265	84.0
Virginia	375,799	85.0
North Carolina	240,309	83.1
South Carolina	115,480	82.4
New Jersey	98,620	58.0
Delaware	39,966	86.3
Georgia	43,948	83.1
New Hampshire	132,726	94.1
Massachusetts Bay . .	354,528	95.0
Rhode Island	69,079	96.0
Connecticut	223,437	96.2
New York	245,901	78.2
Pennsylvania	249,656	59.0

5. *The English Influence on American Life*

America's first colonists gave English names to many of their villages and towns, to geographic features such as rivers and capes, and to most of the new colonies. With few exceptions, these names became permanent and are still used today. Examples of such names given to villages and towns are Plymouth, Salem, Marblehead, Norfolk, Boston, Waterton, Portsmouth, Albany, New London, and York. English names given to geographic sites were the Thames River, Cape Fear, Cape Hatteras, Cape Cod, Cape Glouster, the James River, and the York River.

English names were given to most of the colonies. Virginia was named for Elizabeth, the "virgin queen." Maryland was named for Maria, the wife of Charles I, and Georgia for King George I. New York was named for James, the Duke of York and brother of King Charles II. New Jersey was named for the Isle of Jersey in the English Channel and Pennsylvania for William Penn. Maine was derived from the English word "mainland," and Delaware was named for Thomas West, Lord De La Warr.

A street in Plymouth, Massachusetts in the middle of the 19th century.

A large number of traditional English family names were introduced into the American colonies, especially by the early settlers. These names were handed down from generation to generation, and many of them became among the most commonly used family names in American society. There is scarcely a community today in the United States in which a number of these names are not present. The origin of these names is interesting. For example, some were derived from forenames such as Williams, Davies, Thomas, Evans, Charles, Morgan, Allan, Price, Phillips, Watson, Bennett, Griffiths, Roberts, Johnson, David, Martin, Morris, and James.

A large number of English names were based on common occupations. Examples of such names are Smith, Taylor, Weaver, Tyler, Farmer, Wainwright, Carpenter, Cartwright, Tanner, Miller, and Tinker. Others were related to rank such as Bishop, Priest, Rector, Chaplain, Deacon, Cannon, Earl, Squire, Sheriff, Major, Sergeant, Prentice, Bailey, and Masters. Some of these names were based on descriptive adjectives such as Young, Black, Brown, Reid (Red), Strong, Short, Long, Longman, Longfellow, Little, Armstrong, Meek, Elder, and Fairhead.

Other English names were derived from the names of places. Some of these are Sutton, York, Middleton, Dorset, Kent, English,

Scott, and Walsh. Still another group of family names were taken from topographical features such as Lake, Rivers, Hill, Dale, Shores, Brooks, Ford, Woods, Banks, Dykes, Parks, Glenn, and Forest. Even nicknames supplied a few family names such as Drinkwater, Lovelady, Lovejoy, and Makepeace.

The colonists who settled from Massachusetts Bay to Georgia brought with them the traditions and customs of English life. Some of these changed gradually, due to a new environment, but society remained basically English during this colonial period. The colonists used England's system of government and its language, laws, dress, architecture, literature, religion, and common social practices. Groups of non-English immigrants settled in the colonies from time to time. The largest of these were the Scotch-Irish, Dutch, French, Germans, and Swedes. However, they never became numerous enough to greatly change the basic English culture present in the colonies. Eventually, they adopted the language, dress, and general social customs of the English majority.

In law and government, the English background of the colonists proved especially important. From England, the Americans became familiar with the English common law, trial by jury, and the idea of representative government. English political writers, especially the philosopher John Locke, were widely read in the colonies. Locke argued that a good monarchy consisted of a "contract" between a king and his subjects in which powers and also responsibilities on both sides were recognized and defined. If followed, this would always prevent tyranny, for no people would willingly give a king unlimited power. Locke's ideas became very popular in the colonies during the 18th century. They played a basic part in creating the critical attitude toward England that brought on the American Revolution.

Pocahantas and John Smith. According to legend, John Smith, leader of the Jamestown colony, was saved from death by Pocahantas, the daughter of the Indian chief, Powhatan. Later, Pocahantas married one of the Virginia settlers.

6. *Prominent Colonial Leaders of English Descent*

The colonies produced a number of famous men during the colonial period. Many of these leaders were of English origin because of the high proportion of English settlers in the colonies.

The first group of prominent colonial figures included the men who established the early colonies. Captain John Smith of Virginia, though not an official leader, belongs in this group. Captain Smith took over control of the colony when the colonists wished to return to England after a bad harvest. By severe measures such as "no work, no food," Smith saved the colonists from famine, and thus guaranteed the future of the colony. Captain

John Winthrop was chosen governor by the Massachusetts Bay colonists before they left England. Winthrop ruled the colony with a strong hand until 1649.

Smith also established friendly relations with the neighboring Indians.

Cecil Calvert, who founded the colony of Maryland, won recognition for his policy of religious toleration. Though Maryland was a Catholic colony, Calvert sponsored a Toleration Act in the Maryland assembly in 1649. This gave complete religious liberty to all who confessed the Christian religion. John Winthrop, the first governor of Massachusetts Bay, became noted for the courage with which he met the early problems of that colony. Reverend

Penn's Treaty with the Indians, a painting by Benjamin West. From the very beginning of his Pennsylvania colony, Penn treated the Indians fairly and kindly. For this reason, Pennsylvania was spared from Indian attacks during Penn's lifetime.

Thomas Hooker, who personally led a group of followers overland from Boston to the Connecticut Valley, became well-known for establishing the colony of Connecticut. Reverend Roger Williams won prominence for founding the colony of Rhode Island. Since Williams had been driven out of Massachusetts Bay because of his religious views, he insisted that the colony of Rhode Island be extremely liberal in all matters of religion. Church and state were completely separated in Rhode Island, and the government was based on the "free consent of all free inhabitants."

The founders of two other colonies, Penn of Pennsylvania and Oglethorpe of Georgia, were known as outstanding liberals. Although Penn established Pennsylvania as a haven for persecuted Quakers, he insisted on complete religious freedom for all his colonists. Penn was also fair to the Indians. He was careful to purchase from them, at a good price, all the land that was occupied by his settlers. As a result of this policy, Pennsylvania was spared all the horrors of Indian warfare during the lifetime of William Penn. James Oglethorpe, as we have noted, founded Georgia to give English debtors a second chance. The English government and prison authorities, however, did not cooperate with Oglethorpe

James Oglethorpe, founder of the colony of Georgia. In colonial times, thousands of Englishmen were imprisoned for personal debts. Oglethorpe planned an American colony where these men could begin life anew.

after he reached America, and his plan to establish a debtor's colony failed. Oglethorpe's great humanitarian goal, however, was never forgotten.

Besides those who founded colonies, a group of colonists of English descent won renown by their contributions in the fields of literature, art, and science. Literature in the colonial period consisted mainly of local histories, and essays and books pertaining to religion. The best of the colonial histories were William Bradford's *History of Plymouth Plantation* and John Winthrop's *A History of New England.* Among the best known religious writers was Roger Williams of Rhode Island who defended religious liberty. Increase Mather and his son, Cotton, of Massachusetts, wrote essays on various sacred topics. Jonathan Edwards, also of Massachusetts, wrote many books in support of Puritanism.

After 1700, a group of colonists became well-known for their accomplishments in art and science. Several artists of exceptional ability appeared. The most famous were Benjamin West and Charles Willson Peale. West had a most interesting career. After several years of successful portrait painting in America, he moved to London where he was the official court painter of the English

George Washington at Princeton (*left*) and **Benjamin Franklin** (*right*), both painted by Charles Willson Peale, one of the most famous artists of the late colonial period.

court. Peale, on the other hand, did not leave the colonies. His portraits included many of the most prominent colonial leaders. Some of his famous pictures are studies of George Washington. The most noted colonial scientist was Benjamin Franklin. Franklin's scientific accomplishments and writings were known throughout Europe. His greatest achievements were his work with electricity and his many inventions.

7. *The American Revolution*

From 1700 to 1763, the American colonists became increasingly critical of the policies England used in governing her American possessions. The mother country's regulation of trade and the direct taxation that was placed on the colonists led to the American Revolution which began in 1775. Some of the most outspoken leaders of this revolt were colonists of English descent, such as Samuel Adams and James Otis. Adams was a fiery, unyielding patriot. His speeches and actions aroused violent resistance to

England throughout Massachusetts. James Otis encouraged rebellion by a series of pamphlets which challenged British control of colonial trade.

On the American side, the Revolutionary War was conducted chiefly by officers of direct English descent. The best known of these was General George Washington, the commander-in-chief of all the American forces. Washington's military skill and stubborn spirit eventually won independence for the colonies after seven and one-half years of war. Other noted officers of English blood in the colonial forces were General Horatio Gates, who captured an entire British army in the battle of Saratoga, and General Nathaniel Greene, who won major victories in the southern colonies.

Samuel Adams (*left*) was the leader of the Massachusetts assembly which opposed England's regulation of trade. Later, he called for revolution and independence. **James Otis** (*right*) was a noted lawyer who objected to the Stamp Act and argued that taxation without representation violated the English constitution.

General Horatio Gates (*left*). The striking victory of General Gates at Saratoga, New York, resulted in the capture of an entire British army. It also encouraged France to enter the war as an ally of the American colonies. **General Nathaniel Greene** (*right*), at one time a Quaker blacksmith from Rhode Island, commanded the American forces in the southern colonies.

Not all of the English colonists were American patriots, however. Thousands objected to the break with the mother country. These people were called Tories by the patriots. Many of them spied for the British, sold them supplies, and joined the British forces. Towards the end of the war, thousands of Tories left the country. Most of them settled in Canada.

PART III.

English Immigration to the United States

1. *Immigration from 1789 to 1860*

For the first few years after the close of the Revolutionary War, immigration from England to America practically stopped. Very few English immigrants landed in any American port between 1783 and 1789. This rapid decline in immigration from England was due chiefly to British hostility toward America because of the Revolutionary War. After 1789, when the government of the United States was established, some immigration from England reappeared. But not until after 1815 did its volume equal that of the colonial period.

Early in the 1790's, a relatively small but continuous migration of farm laborers from England to America began. This resulted from a shortage of farmland in England at that time. About 1795, a large group of skilled workmen began to arrive from England to find jobs in the new textile mills being built in New England and New Jersey. Previously, the owners of these mills had sent agents to England to recruit skilled textile laborers for their new plants. Thousands of textile workers arrived in America during the late 1790's in response to this appeal.

Calico printing in a New England textile mill. Many of the English immigrants that came to America in the 19th century found work in textile mills.

Textile laborers continued to arrive in the United States until 1803. In that year, England and France drifted into a prolonged war which lasted until 1815. This struggle caused all shipping to be used for war purposes, and from 1803 to 1815 practically all immigration from England to America ceased.

With the end of hostilities between England and France, normal immigration from England to America was resumed. From 1815 to 1860, approximately three-quarters of a million immigrants from England reached the United States.

There were three different reasons for this growing immigration from England to America during these years. The first was a gradual and continuous increase in England's population following 1815. The second was the development of the factory system after the return of peace in 1815. Thousands of Englishmen were poverty-stricken by the removal of their traditional source of income, the making of various articles by hand in their own homes. The third reason was a sharp drop in the cost of ocean transportation to the United States following 1820. Between 1815 and 1820, the number of English ships engaged in travel to and from America increased from 300 to 1000. On each voyage from the United States to England, these vessels carried a full cargo of cotton, tobacco, and lumber. On the return trip to America, however, much of the cargo space was not needed for goods and could be used to accommodate passengers. This situation reduced the price of a single passage to the United States from $60 in 1815 to $15 in 1820. Transportation to America was now within the reach of many of the so-called "poor." It also caused many public officials throughout England to decide to ship unemployed farmers and laborers to the United States rather than continue them on relief.

Most of the English immigrants who came to America between 1815 and 1860 settled in the Northern States. Very few were attracted to the South. Industrial jobs did not exist in the South, which was then dominated by large plantations and Negro slavery. Some of the English immigrants of this period found employment in the textile mills of New England and New Jersey. But most of them had been farm laborers in England, and they became tenant farmers in the North Central States. A small minority of these immigrants had been large landowners and wealthy men in England. They came to America because they believed there were greater opportunities than in Great Britain. These rich immigrants purchased thousands of acres of land. Their objective, apparently, was to establish a number of "English colonies" on the prairies of the Midwest. None of these projects proved successful, however, and before long these wealthy Englishmen "disappeared" in the American population which surrounded them.

2. *English Immigration from 1860 to 1900*

During the American Civil War, immigration from England practically ceased. With the return of peace, however, it resumed at a rapid rate. During the next 30 years, from 1865 to 1895, more English immigrants reached the United States than in any other period in our history. This occurred because of a combination of certain conditions in England, and the appearance of new economic opportunities in America. During the 1870's and early 1880's, England experienced a succession of crop failures. This discouraged many English farmers and agricultural laborers, and vast numbers of them migrated to America at that time.

Dissatisfied farmers who left England were able to find numerous new jobs and opportunities in the United States. The Civil War caused a rapid increase in manufacturing in the Northern States to meet the needs of the Union Army and Navy. This industrial growth did not stop with the conclusion of the war, but continued during the remainder of the 1860's, the 1870's, and the 1880's. Thousands of new employees were needed as manufacturing and transportation expanded. At this same time, the settled area in the United States was being advanced westward from the Mississippi River to the Rocky Mountains. This offered excellent opportunities for English immigrants who had been farmers, or farm laborers, to acquire land on the western prairies at very reasonable prices. The combination of industrial and agricultural opportunities caused more than two and one-third million Englishmen to settle in the United States between 1860 and 1895. The peak of this large-scale immigration was 1888, when some 200,000 English immigrants arrived at American ports.

A third reason for the extensive English immigration to the United States following the Civil War was a marked improvement in ocean transportation. Shortly after 1865, steamships began to replace sailing vessels in trans-Atlantic passenger service. This reduced the length of an average Atlantic crossing from nearly two months to about 15 or 18 days. These new rapid crossings not only increased the number of passengers that could be transported in a single year, but they also reduced the inconvenience and the high incidence of illness and death caused by longer voyages.

Following 1875, English immigrants were attracted to America by an extensive advertising campaign conducted by American businesses. For example, United States steamship companies placed large advertisements in English newspapers which described the speed, pleasure, and low cost of an ocean trip to the United States. American railroad companies, whose tracks ran from the Ohio Valley to the Pacific coast, also advertised extensively in England. These companies needed new immigrants to settle on vacant land along their rights-of-way in the upper Midwest and Northwest. In addition to placing ads in newspapers, the railroad companies sent many personal agents to England. They passed out handbills, pamphlets, and maps to discontented farmers and factory workers. This material told how the railroad companies would pay transportation costs to America for prospective immigrants. It also described how cheaply land could be purchased in mid-America, and how railroad companies would guarantee long-term mortgages. Even state and territorial governments, from Wisconsin to Oregon, sent agents to England to encourage immigrants to settle within their own borders.

Of the immigrants between 1870 and 1896, a quarter of a million found employment in factories and mills along the Atlantic coast. Most of these had been industrial workers in England. About 2,000,000 of the total English immigration of that period settled on farms in the upper Midwest and the far West. Thousands of newly-arrived Englishmen moved into the farming areas of Wisconsin, Iowa, Nebraska, North and South Dakota, and the fertile river valleys of Oregon and Washington. Having been farmers in England, these immigrants soon learned how to grow crops on the western prairies. Because of their energy and pride, many of them owned their own farms within a few years. Already speaking the English language, and having a culture very similar to that of America, these English immigrants rapidly merged into the large American population that surrounded them.

3. *Immigration from 1900 to 1920*

About 1900, emigration from England began to follow a different pattern than during the 19th century. Between 1800 and 1900, English emigrants had gone almost exclusively to the United States. Early in the 20th century, however, many English emigrants began to go to various parts of the British Empire such as Canada, Australia, New Zealand, and South Africa.

IMMIGRATION FROM GREAT BRITAIN*
Source: Immigration and Naturalization Service

1821-1830	25,079
1831-1840	75,810
1841-1850	267,044
1851-1860	423,974
1861-1870	606,896
1871-1880	548,043
1881-1890	807,357
1891-1900	271,538
1901-1910	525,950
1911-1920	341,408
1921-1930	340,780
1931-1940	31,572
1941-1950	139,306
1951-1960	204,468
1961-1970	214,518
1971-1980	137,374

*These figures include immigrants from England, Wales, Scotland, and, after 1925, Northern Ireland. About 80 to 90 percent are English.

Immigrants arriving at Ellis Island in New York about 1900. Many immigrants were encouraged to come to America because of the advertising by steamship lines and railroad companies.

In spite of this change, large numbers of Englishmen continued to immigrate to the United States. Between 1900 and 1914, more than 800,000 English immigrants reached America. Most of these were factory workers who were unemployed because of a depression that began in English industry in 1903. These immigrants found work in factories, plants, and mills along the eastern coast, and in the growing steel empires in northern Indiana and Ohio. Speaking English and being familiar with American customs, the English immigrants rapidly disappeared into the surrounding population. So smoothly did this occur that their arrival attracted no attention on the national scene.

The First World War began in June 1914 and ended in November 1918. During that time there was practically no immigration from England to the United States, for two basic reasons. One was that British industry was engaged in a war effort which created jobs for all the English laboring class. This meant that there were no idle workers in Britain during the war years, and thus few were interested in seeking employment overseas. The second reason was that all British shipping was engaged in war activities and no vessels were available for immigrant transportation.

4. *Immigration Following 1920*

After World War I, the United States withdrew from Europe, rejected membership in the League of Nations, and adopted a policy of isolation in foreign affairs. This attitude was reflected in the field of immigration by the passage of the Immigration Act of 1921, the first American law which greatly restricted new immigration. In 1924, Congress passed a law setting a fixed number, or quota, for immigration from each country. Another act was passed in 1929 which set the number of immigrants allowed to enter the United States annually at 150,000. These were to be divided among foreign countries on the basis of the national origins of our population as shown by the census of 1890. For example, a country that did not send a large number of immigrants to America before 1890, would now only be allowed to send a very limited number. England had sent a large number of immigrants to America prior to 1890 and therefore did not suffer as much from the quota system as many other countries of the world.

From 1921 through 1928, an average of 35,000 English immigrants entered the United States annually. In 1929, the national origins quota came into effect, and England was allowed to send a maximum of 65,721 immigrants to America each year. This was the largest single quota set for any foreign country. In the future, however, the great depression of the 1930's, and World War II, which lasted from 1939 to 1945, seriously interferred with all European immigration to the United States. During this period England did not use more than one-third of her annual quota of immigrants entitled to enter the United States. In later years, from 1951 to the mid-1960's, the number of English immigrants who reached American ports did not exceed 25,000.

The quota system of immigration was abandoned as American policy when new legislation was passed in 1965. The new system, which took effect June 30, 1968, set an annual limit of 120,000 immigrants from North and South America and 170,000 from the rest of the world. In 1978, the hemisphere limits were replaced with a worldwide limit of 290,000 immigrants per year.

PART IV.

Contributions of English-Americans

1. *The Adoption of the Constitution of the United States*

The American Revolution ended in 1783 by an agreement between England and America known as the Treaty of Paris. By the provisions of this document, England granted independence to its former American colonies.

Between 1783 and 1789, the 13 American states were governed by a document called the Articles of Confederation. This established a loose alliance, or confederacy, with an extremely weak form of government. No executive branch existed, such as the Presidency. The government consisted only of a Congress composed of one house. The various states were extremely jealous of the central government, and they kept most of the basic powers in their own hands. Congress had no authority to levy taxes, and the only income of the central government consisted of gifts, or donations, by the states. The American government had no army or navy under its direct control, and lacking strength, it was not respected by other countries at that time.

Washington Addressing the Constitutional Convention. Washington's great fame as a patriot and military hero enabled him to guide the sessions of the Constitutional Convention to a successful conclusion. Later, he was unanimously elected to be the first President of the new United States.

Gradually, between 1783 and 1789, the merchant, landowning, and banking classes began to demand a stronger form of government. In May 1787, a convention of delegates from the various states met at Philadelphia for the purpose of strengthening the Articles of Confederation. A total of 55 delegates assembled. The majority of these delegates were of direct English descent. Most of their ancestors had originally come to America at the beginning of the colonial period. The most prominent delegates were: George Washington, James Madison, and Edmund Randolph from Virginia; Benjamin Franklin and Robert Morris from Pennsylvania; Oliver Ellsworth from Connecticut; William Patterson from New Jersey; John Dickinson from Delaware; Charles Pinckney from South Carolina; Rufus King from Massachusetts.

Shortly after the convention opened, the delegates realized that a different form of government was needed. Finally, after weeks of discussion and argument, the convention adjourned in September 1787. A new constitution had been written and adopted which established a government known as the United States of America. The next step was for the states to ratify, or approve, this constitution. Ratification by nine states was required. Between September 1787 and June 1788, nine states gradually gave their approval to the new Constitution of the United States. The leaders of the Philadelphia convention led the fight for ratification throughout the country. Some made extensive speaking tours. Others wrote pamphlets and essays which explained the advantages of the new Constitution. Thus, our present United States Constitution was written, and its ratification secured, largely by Americans of English origin.

2. *Presidents of English Descent*

In November 1788, a national election was held to choose electors who would select the first President. As a result of this election, George Washington became our first Chief Executive. Altogether, 21 men of English heritage have served as Presidents of the United States. Several of these Presidents, however, have been of mixed descent and are not solely of English origin. They also have Scottish, Scotch-Irish, German, or French ancestors. They are, therefore, sometimes found in other lists of the national origins of our Presidents. This group with mixed ancestry includes Andrew Johnson, Ulysses S. Grant, Grover Cleveland, Lyndon B. Johnson, and Jimmy Carter.

George Washington (1732-1799) first studied to be a surveyor. When he inherited the estate at Mount Vernon, he became a planter. Washington began his military career in the Virginia militia and later served in the French and Indian War. His service as Commander-in-Chief of the Continental Army helped unite the colonies into one nation. In 1789 he was elected the first President of the United States and served two terms. Largely because of his leadership, the states survived their first uncertain years as a nation. This portrait is by Gilbert Stuart, one of the great early American painters.

Presidents of English Descent

Number	Name	Year of Inauguration	Number	Name	Year of Inauguration
1st	George Washington	1789	18th	Ulysses S. Grant	1869
2nd	John Adams	1797	20th	James A. Garfield	1881
4th	James Madison	1809	22nd	Grover Cleveland	1885
6th	John Quincy Adams	1825	23rd	Benjamin Harrison	1889
9th	William H. Harrison	1841	27th	William H. Taft	1909
10th	John Tyler	1841	29th	Warren G. Harding	1921
12th	Zachary Taylor	1849	30th	Calvin Coolidge	1923
13th	Millard Fillmore	1850	33rd	Harry S. Truman	1945
14th	Franklin Pierce	1853	36th	Lyndon B. Johnson	1963
16th	Abraham Lincoln	1861	39th	James Earl Carter, Jr.	1977
17th	Andrew Johnson	1865			

John Adams (1735-1826) *left*, was a member of the famous Adams family of Braintree, Massachusetts. Adams began his career as a lawyer. He was a member of the First and Second Continental Congress, and served as Vice-President under George Washington. Charles Willson Peale painted this portrait.

James Madison (1751-1836) *right*, a son of a Virginia planter, spent most of his life in public service. Madison was a member of the Continental Congress and his work in the Constitutional Convention won him the name "father of the Constitution." He held the office of President for eight years, and later helped Thomas Jefferson establish the University of Virginia.

John Quincy Adams (1767-1848) *right,* son of John Adams, was the sixth President of the United States. Like his father, Adams had a long career in public service. He served as a diplomat to several countries, a United States senator, and Secretary of State before being elected to the Presidency.

William Henry Harrison (1773-1841) *left,* was the son of a prominent colonial family of Virginia. His career as a frontiersman and a famous Indian fighter at the Battle of Tippecanoe made him a colorful candidate for the Presidency. The campaign slogan of Harrison and his running mate, John Tyler, "Tippecanoe and Tyler, too," became a famous phrase. On his inauguration day, Harrison caught cold and died of pneumonia one month later.

John Tyler (1790-1862) *right,* was the first Vice-President to complete the President's term in office. Although Tyler had a long political career, he was disliked as President. As a result, little was accomplished during his years in office.

Zachary Taylor (1784-1850) *left*, a war hero nicknamed "Old Rough and Ready" by his men, served as the 12th President of the United States. Taylor fought in the Indian Wars, the War of 1812, and the Mexican War. As President, Taylor upheld the Constitution and the Union at a time when slavery was becoming a national crisis, even though he was a Southerner and a slaveholder. He died in 1850, after 16 months in office.

Millard Fillmore (1800-1874) *right*, became President of the United States at the death of Zachary Taylor in 1850. He grew up in New York State, and educated himself with the help of his wife, a schoolteacher. His political career included five terms as a member of the United States House of Representatives.

Franklin Pierce (1804-1869) *left*, was born in New Hampshire, the son of the governor of that state. He interrupted his political career to serve in the Mexican War. As President, he tended to side with the Southern cause of slavery. Thus, he lost the support of many Northern voters and served only one term in office.

Abraham Lincoln (1809-1865) rose from a self-educated backwoods boy to President of the United States. He believed that his main purpose as President during the Civil War was to save the Union, and he faced great criticism in both the North and the South. He is probably best remembered for freeing the slaves by the Emancipation Proclamation, his Gettysburg Address, and his love of humanity. Lincoln was assassinated in 1865. Had he lived and been able to carry out his plans for healing the nation after the war, Reconstruction might not have been such a dark period in American history.

Andrew Johnson (1808-1875) *left,* the son of parents of both English and Scottish descent, served as President after Lincoln's death. Johnson was opposed by a group of radicals in Congress who wished to punish the Southerners. In 1868, after much conflict between the President and the Congress, Johnson became the only President to be impeached. He was later acquitted and allowed to finish his term in office.

James Garfield (1831-1881) *right,* the son of pioneer settlers in Ohio, struggled hard to obtain an education. His determination and efforts paid off, for he became president of Hiram College in Ohio, a major general in the Civil War, and a United States Congressman. Garfield was assassinated in 1881, only four months after his inauguration as President.

Ulysses S. Grant (1882-1885) *below,* met with many successes and failures during his lifetime. A West Point graduate, Grant served in the Mexican War and then resigned from the Army. After several years of failure as a farmer and businessman, Grant returned to military service and became a national hero in the Civil War. He was elected President, but because of a lack of experience in politics, was unable to solve many of the problems that arose during his two terms in office.

51

Grover Cleveland (1837-1908) *right*, was a President of English and Scotch-Irish descent. During his political career, he served as mayor of Buffalo, New York, and governor of New York State. Cleveland was the first man to serve two inconsecutive terms as President. He was also the first President to be married in the White House.

Benjamin Harrison (1833-1901) *left*, was the grandson of William Henry Harrison. Harrison served as an officer in the Civil War and was later elected United States senator from Indiana. During his term as President, the United States was still in the period of expansion. The Oklahoma Territory was opened to settlers and six states were admitted to the Union.

William Howard Taft (1857-1930) *right*, son of a successful lawyer and attorney general under President Grant, had a long political career. Some of his positions were governor general of the Philippine Islands, Secretary of War, and provisional governor of Cuba. After one term as President, he served as Chief Justice of the Supreme Court. His wife, Helen Taft, was responsible for planting the famous Japanese cherry trees in Washington.

Warren G. Harding (1865-1923), born and raised in Ohio, began his career as a newspaper editor. He served as a state senator in Ohio, and later as a United States senator. Although Harding tried to do a good job as President, some of the men he appointed to office were not honest and involved him in scandals. Harding died in office in 1923.

Calvin Coolidge (1872-1933) was the son of New England parents. He held several offices in the State of Massachusetts, including governor. Coolidge became President at the death of Harding in 1923. He cleared up the scandals of Harding's administration and was elected President in his own right in 1924.

53

Harry S. Truman (1884-1972) was raised as a farm boy in Missouri. After serving in World War I, he entered politics and later was elected United States senator. In 1944, Truman was elected Vice-President and the following year became President at the death of Franklin Roosevelt. During his two terms as President, World War II ended, the United Nations was created, and the Korean War began.

Lyndon B. Johnson (1908-1973) became the 36th President of the United States after the tragic death of John F. Kennedy in 1963. The son of parents of English and Scottish descent, Johnson was a teacher before entering politics. He was elected to the House of Representatives in 1938 and to the Senate in 1948, where he served for many years before becoming Vice-President.

James Earl Carter, Jr, (1924-   ) has English ancestors who first settled in America in 1635. Before entering politics, Jimmy Carter managed a farm in Georgia. After serving as a Georgia state senator, he was elected governor of that state. In 1976 he ran for the presidency, campaigning for reform and new openness in government. In 1977 he took office as the 39th President of the United States.

54

3. *Prominent English-American Families*

A number of families of English origin that trace their roots back to colonial times have contributed a great deal to American history. Perhaps the most prominent was the Adams family. Its American history began when Henry Adams settled in Braintree, or modern Quincy, Massachusetts, in 1636. During the colonial period, the Adams family produced a number of clergymen and educators prominent in the history of Massachusetts. In the 1760's, the spark of rebellion against England was ignited and fanned throughout New England by the fiery pen and voice of Samuel Adams, the father of the American Revolution. Later, the Adams family produced two Presidents of the United States. John Adams served as the second President from 1797-1801, and John Quincy Adams as the sixth President from 1825-1829. Other members of the Adams family who achieved prominence were: Charles Francis Adams, the United States Ambassador to England during the Civil War; William Adams, the leading Presbyterian clergyman in America in the 19th century; Charles Kendall Adams, a well-known educator following the Civil War; and Henry Brooks Adams, a renowned historian in the latter part of the 19th century.

The Byrd family has produced a number of prominent Americans. William Byrd settled in Virginia in 1674. During the colonial period, many of the Byrds were large landowners and well-known politicians in Virginia. In the twentieth century, Admiral Richard E. Byrd won fame as a naval officer and explorer of both the North and South poles. Senator Harry S. Byrd was nationally known as a powerful conservative Democrat.

The Lodge and Cabot families produced many men of prominence during the colonial history of Massachusetts. These two families were founded by English immigrants who settled in New

In 1926, **Admiral Richard E. Byrd** made the first airplane flight to the North Pole. In 1929, he was the first to fly over the South Pole. He combined the careers of naval officer, explorer, and scientist.

Amy Lowell (1874-1925) was a poet noted for her experiments with free verse and imagery. Two of her most famous works are *Sword Blades and Poppy Seeds*, a book of poems, and her excellent biography, *John Keats*.

Robert Traill Spence Lowell, Jr. (1917-1977) won the Pulitzer prize for poetry twice —in 1947 for *Lord Weary's Castle*, and in 1974 for *The Dolphin*. During the 1960's, he was politically active as an anti-war protester.

England in the 1640's. At the end of World War I, Senator Henry Cabot Lodge of Massachusetts won a prominent role in American history by opposing the United States' entrance in the League of Nations. His grandson, also named Henry Cabot Lodge, served in the Senate and was twice ambassador to South Vietnam.

The Lowell family first came to Massachusetts from England in 1639. Their descendants entered successfully into a wide range of pursuits. In the early 1800's, Francis Cabot Lowell established the first cotton mill in New England and founded the industrial town of Lowell, Massachusetts. One of the most influential family members was James Russell Lowell (1819-1891), in whom were combined the talents of poet, editor, literary critic, teacher, social reformer, and diplomat. Among other activities he taught at Harvard University, edited the *Atlantic Monthly*, and served as United States minister to Spain and England. His cousin, Amy Lowell, was a noted poet and critic. In 1894 another prominent family member, astronomer Percival Lowell, founded the famous Lowell Observatory in Flagstaff, Arizona. A distinguished Lowell who lived in more recent times was Robert Lowell, one of America's leading modern poets.

4. *Literature*

The names of Americans of English descent shine through the history of American literature. This is not unnatural. Immigrants from non-English-speaking countries could and did rise to prominence in many fields of life. But literature requires an intimate grasp of language, and the immigrant from the non-English-speaking world was at a disadvantage. The disadvantage could persist for a generation or even longer. Perhaps this explains why most of our classic American authors, and some of our great contemporary writers, are of English origin.

The first half of the 19th century saw a flowering of American literature, especially in New England. All of these authors were descendants of English immigrants who had settled in Massachusetts and Connecticut between 1630 and 1660.

Nathaniel Hawthorne, author of *The Scarlet Letter,* was descended from ancestors who came from Binfield, England, in 1630 and settled in Dorchester, Massachusetts.

The forefathers of Henry David Thoreau, author of *Walden,* were mainly English and had migrated from the Isle of Jersey.

Ralph Waldo Emerson, most famous for his *Essays,* was English on both sides. The first Emerson settled at Ipswich, Massachusetts, in 1635.

Oliver Wendell Holmes, physician, poet, and essayist, was mainly English in lineage. He was descended from an ancestor who settled at Woodstock, Massachusetts, in the 1640's. Another Oliver Wendell Homes, the oldest son of the writer, became a

Ralph Waldo Emerson *(left),* a philosopher, essayist, and poet, urged men to study nature, to do their own thinking, and to seek God in everything that surrounded them.

Edgar Allan Poe *(right)* wrote poems and stories of mystery and terror.

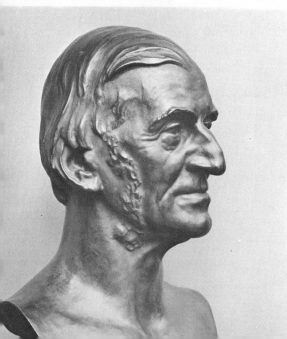
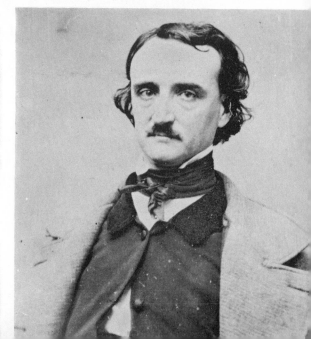

justice of the Supreme Court of the United States and one of our most influential jurists.

Edgar Allan Poe, a well-known poet and short story writer, was the son of an English actress.

Henry Wadsworth Longfellow, the author of *Hiawatha* and *Evangeline,* was descended from Edward Longfellow who came to Massachusetts from Yorkshire, England, in the 1640's.

John Greenleaf Whittier, the poet, traced his English heritage to Thomas Whittier, who migrated from England to Massachusetts in 1638.

Walt Whitman, author of *Leaves of Grass,* was descended from Joseph Whitman who left England in the 1660's and settled in Stratford, Connecticut.

Emily Dickinson, a poetess who attained fame only after her death, was part of an old New England family that was English in origin.

Samuel Clemens, who is best known by his pen name, Mark Twain, was descended from an old Virginia family that came from England. Twain will be famous as long as boys are like *Tom Sawyer* and *Huckleberry Finn.*

Among modern American writers of English descent, one returned to the England from which his ancestors had come. T. S. Eliot, poet, dramatist, and literary critic, was of Massachusetts Puritan stock. He left the United States in the 1920's to settle in England, and died in 1965. He was awarded the Nobel prize for literature in 1948.

Robert Frost, one of America's best loved poets, was descended from Scottish and English immigrants to New England. During his lifetime Frost won the Pulitzer prize for poetry four times and was awarded a gold medal by the United States Congress.

William Faulkner, the noted novelist who received the Nobel prize for literature in 1949, was descended from a Mississippi pioneer family which originated in England.

Tennessee Williams, one of our most prominent playwrights, descended from Tennessee pioneer stock which was mainly of English origin. He twice won the Pulitzer prize for drama. This award was given to him in 1948 for his play *A Streetcar Named Desire* and in 1955 for his *Cat on a Hot Tin Roof.*

5. *Invention*

The 19th century saw a number of important inventions that greatly influenced American life. Three of these were the work of Americans of English origin. The first English-American inventor of note was Eli Whitney. He was a New England schoolteacher who moved to Georgia about 1790 to improve his health. After arriving there, he noticed how slowly cotton was prepared for market by handpicking the seeds from the raw cotton, and decided that a better method could be found. After some experimentation he invented the cotton gin. This increased by 300 times the volume of cotton that could be seeded in one day by one Negro slave.

A model of the cotton gin, invented by Eli Whitney. The cotton gin greatly reduced the long period of time required to remove the seeds from raw cotton. Thus, cotton became the most profitable crop of the South.

Before long, cotton became the most profitable product produced in the South. Another result of Whitney's invention, however, was the South's increased dependence on Negro slavery. Largely because of Whitney's invention, slavery continued in the Southern States until the Civil War.

Another English-American inventor who became famous during the 19th century was Samuel F. Morse. In 1837, Morse became interested in sending electric impulses over a copper wire. By the use of a code, letters and words could be transmitted in this fashion. It took Morse until 1844 to perfect his method of sending messages, but the telegraph had been born. In a public demonstration at Washington, D.C. that same year, Morse sent a message to Baltimore which proved the success of his invention. The telegraph immediately became of tremendous importance in assisting business, the government, the military and naval services, and in relaying information about current events to newspapers, and thus to the general public.

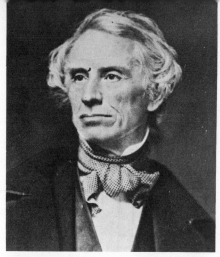

Samuel F. B. Morse, with his invention of the telegraph, helped to revolutionize the world of communication.

Isaac M. Singer, inventor of the sewing machine, the basis for the mass production of clothing.

Isaac M. Singer was an American of English descent who, in the year 1840, invented the sewing machine. This resulted in the mass production of clothing and many other articles made of cloth. A retail clothing business soon appeared which offered ready-to-wear clothes for both men and women.

The 20th century also witnessed the work of important English-American inventors. Orville and Wilbur Wright designed and flew the first airplane at Kitty Hawk, North Carolina in 1903.

Wilbur *(left)* and **Orville Wright** *(right),* the famous aviators of Dayton, Ohio. The Wright brothers first became interested in aviation through the sport of gliding. Later, they constructed and flew the first motor-driven airplane.

The first flight. Wilbur and Orville Wright flew the world's first powered aircraft near Kitty Hawk, North Carolina on December 17, 1903. Wilbur is in the plane, and Orville stands nearby. The spot where the flight occurred is marked by the Wright Brothers National Monument (*right*), the nation's tribute to the two great pioneers in the field of aviation.

Thomas A. Edison, probably the greatest inventor of all time, secured more than 1000 patents during his lifetime. The best known of his inventions were the phonograph, the motion picture, the electric light, and the electric dynamo.

Thomas A. Edison was without doubt the most resourceful inventor in all history. He developed hundreds of inventions which improved practically every aspect of American life.

6. *Military Service*

General George Washington was not the only military leader of English descent that commanded American armies in time of war.

The Civil War's most prominent generals were also descendants of English immigrants, on both the Union and the Confederate side. General Ulysses S. Grant, although of Scotch-Irish extraction on his mother's side, traced his family name back to Matthew Grant, who came from England to Massachusetts in 1630. General Robert E. Lee was of direct English origin.

Commodore Matthew C. Perry of the United States Navy won renown in American history when he led a fleet across the Pacific Ocean and anchored in Tokyo Bay. Up to that time Japan had remained completely isolated from the world. It had no commercial or diplomatic contact with other nations. Perry visited Japan for the purpose of opening diplomatic relations. The Japanese were hostile at first, but Commodore Perry remained firm in his demand for a treaty. Eventually, the Japanese agreed to exchange ambassadors and to open certain Japanese ports to American traders.

Two American generals of English descent were important in World War II. General George C. Marshall directed America's campaigns against Germany and Japan as the United States Army's

The Civil War ended when Lee surrendered his army to Grant at Appomattox Court House in western Virginia on April 9, 1865.

Robert E. Lee *(left)*, commander of the Confederate Army. Lee was the son of General Henry Lee who had fought under Washington during the Revolution. Although Lee was disturbed about fighting against the United States, he felt that it was his duty to serve his native state of Virginia.

Commodore Matthew Perry *(right)*. He won a major diplomatic victory by urging Japan, after 200 years of isolation, to open its ports to American traders.

Chief of Staff. Later, under President Truman, General Marshall served as Secretary of State and was the author of the famous "Marshall Plan" for the reconstruction of war-destroyed Europe. General James Doolittle led an air force raid on Japan in the early days of World War II. It was a daring act, and did much to raise American morale after Pearl Harbor. It also showed the Japanese that their homeland was not immune from attack.

7. *Industry and Commerce*

In the 1780's, an English textile worker by the name of Samuel Slater immigrated from England to Rhode Island. At that time, the

A stamp issued in 1953 commemorating the 100th anniversary of Commodore Perry's treaty with Japan.

machinery in an English textile mill was a carefully guarded secret. Before Slater left England, he memorized the design of the machines in the mill where he was employed. Then after he reached New England, he secured the help of some businessmen and built a duplicate of an English spinning mill in southern Rhode Island. This plant began production in 1790. Because of Slater's enterprise, a large and profitable textile industry developed in later years throughout New England and the Southern States.

Colonel Edwin L. Drake founded America's oil industry. In 1859, Drake developed the world's first oil well in the mountains of western Pennsylvania. From crude oil, refined oil was soon produced and then numerous by-products such as gasoline which shortly helped revolutionize industry and transportation.

James J. Hill was a railroad tycoon known as the "empire builder." He constructed and directed the Great Northern railroad. This line opened up settlement from Minnesota to the Pacific Northwest.

The Marshall Field family of Chicago is also of English descent. The first Marshall Field founded the store bearing his name, which is one of the world's great department stores. The Field family today is important in newspaper and book publishing, real estate developing, and manufacturing, in addition to merchandising.

Frank Lloyd Wright (1869-1959) was one of the great architects of the 20th century, and his work and influence have world recognition. This photo shows him beside the only example of his architecture to be built in New York City, the Solomon R. Guggenheim Museum of Art.

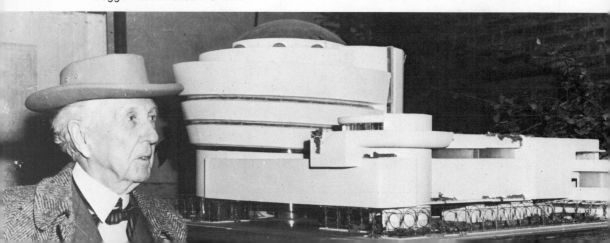

8. *Education, Scholarship, Medicine*

The contributions of Americans of English origin to education and science are enormous. We will mention here only a few examples of people who have done important work in these fields.

James B. Conant, an outstanding American educator, served as president of Harvard University from 1933 to 1953. Later appointed as U. S. ambassador to West Germany and as an educational consultant for the Ford Foundation, Dr. Conant's many books on educational theory and practice have had a great influence on modern American education.

Scholar Charles A. Beard was outstanding among American historians. His books on United States history, such as *An Economic Interpretation of the Constitution* and *The Rise of American Civilization*, are classic works.

Noah Webster was another important scholar of English descent. In 1828 he published his famous *Webster's Dictionary.* We still use modernized versions of his dictionary today. Another Webster of English origin—Daniel Webster—was a great American lawyer, senator, and orator, and a Secretary of State in the administrations of presidents Harrison, Tyler, and Fillmore.

In the field of American medicine, the Mayo brothers are notable. They built the hospital and clinic at Rochester, Minnesota, which bears their name. It is world famous as a center of medical research and treatment.

Dr. William James Mayo *(left),* 1861-1939, and his brother **Dr. Charles Horace Mayo** *(right),* 1865-1939. The Mayo brothers were internationally renowned surgeons. They organized the Mayo Clinic at Rochester, Minnesota in 1889, an institution which attracted patients from the entire world. Both were brigadier generals in the Medical Officers Reserve Corps. They died only two months apart.

Clara Barton was instrumental in founding the American Red Cross.

Jane Addams founded the world-famous Hull House in Chicago.

Another American of English descent who made great contributions to medicine was Clara Barton. She served as a nurse in the American Civil War and the Franco-Prussian War. It was largely through her efforts that the American Red Cross came into being.

Jane Addams was another woman of English ancestry who devoted her life to helping people. In 1888 she founded Hull House, a neighborhood center that provided social services for needy people. She also helped to promote legislative reforms for the protection of working women and children.

9. *Entertainment*

The entertainment world also has its famous members of English origin. Will Rogers, a popular figure in the 1920's, was of English and Indian descent. Rogers always appeared in the role of an Oklahoma cowboy. He combined rope tricks with humorous remarks about politics, current events, and many other subjects.

Some of today's best known entertainers were originally English. Comedian Bob Hope was born Leslie Townes Hope in London. He came to America with his parents at the age of four. Alfred Hitchcock, the movie director famous for his mystery and suspense films, moved to America from his native London in 1939 and became a United States citizen in 1955.

Will Rogers was one of America's best loved humorists.

Cary Grant has been a popular film star for over three decades.

Comedian **Bob Hope** often entertains American troops overseas.

Actor Cary Grant was born Alexander Archibald Leach in Bristol, England. His long and successful movie career began when he moved to the United States in the 1920's. Lynn Fontanne was famous for the stage roles she enacted with her American husband, Alfred Lunt, during the 1930's and 40's. She was born in Essex, England.

English people in America have also made their mark in the field of television. Alistair Cooke, a four-time Emmy Award winner, is best known to many Americans as the host of public television's popular *Masterpiece Theatre*. But he is primarily a journalist and writer. Born in Manchester, England, he now makes his home in New York.

Journalist **Alistair Cooke's** most recent books are *America* and *Six Men*.

Conclusion

Most people in the United States probably have at least some British ancestry. In fact, there are so many prominent Americans of English descent that it has been possible to mention only a few of them in this slim volume.

Today, however, Americans of British ancestry no longer dominate the nation's affairs as they once did. Their influence was at its height in colonial times and during the 19th century. Later, as the United States began to receive vast numbers of immigrants from other countries, people of other heritages came to take a larger share in American life.

Still, the English origins of our United States are deep and permanent. They are found not only in our language, but in the form of our government, our system of law, and our democratic values. The English influence exists at the foundation of our nation, and will persist as long as there is a United States.

ABOUT THE AUTHOR . . .

Dr. Edwin H. Cates, a native of Indiana, obtained his elementary and secondary education there and in Illinois. He later attended the University of Iowa, where he received his A.B., A.M., and his Ph.D. degrees. His field of specialization was American history. After a period as a teacher of social studies at the Martinsville, Illinois high school, he joined the faculty of the Upper Iowa University as an Associate Professor of History. He also held a similar post at Illinois Wesleyan University. In 1946, Dr. Cates was appointed Professor of History at St. Cloud State College, St. Cloud, Minnesota.